THE
BADGE

Irene Reyes-Smith

The Badge© 2023 by Irene Reyes-Smith

Scriptures from various versions of the Bible.

Library of Congress Cataloging– in- Publication Data has been applied for.

Paperback ISBN: 979-8-9885806-5-2

PRINTED IN THE UNITED STATES OF AMERICA.

Permission Granted for Officer Ronald Hampton's Story
Permission Granted for Chief of Police Marcus Jones' Story

FIRST EDITION

Table of Contents

The B.A.D.G.E.

Broken Authority Determining Governing Equality

This story will take you through…
the ups and downs,
the ins and outs, and
the in-between of the badge.

THE
BADGE

In the Beginning

1861 — the year the badge was created. Miriam-Webster Dictionary defines it as a distinctive emblem or token worn as a sign of allegiance, achievement, or authority and awarded for a particular accomplishment. Badges—designed in different shapes, sizes, and forms—are seen by many as a sign of Authority, Acknowledgement, Sacrifice, Safety, and Service. Worn by law enforcement throughout the world, badges represent authority, and all departments have distinctive badges. In some people's eyes, the badge is an aggressive and frightening sign or symbol. But God has given authority to the government and police to uphold the law for good, not evil.

The history of law enforcement and policing is something I'm sure you have heard and read about—or will—during your years of living. Let me provide you with these tidbits if you don't know these already:

1. From the 1800s to the 1980s, hundreds of patrolmen worked out of precincts and had to respond to call boxes to mark their location and answer calls for service.
2. As the history of law enforcement enhanced, patrolmen started being referred to as officers.
3. One-way radio communication came about in the late 1800s. Shortly after, two-way radio communications were implemented for officers on the street, allowing them to communicate with each other and supervisors about their well-being and safety.
4. Around 1970, the precincts transitioned to districts, which now cover certain areas and quadrants of the cities.

In the law enforcement profession, police officers face violence and danger daily. When faced with danger, we must remember God's word:

Have I not commanded you? Be strong and courageous. Do not be afraid; do not be discouraged, for the Lord your God will be with you wherever you go.

Joshua 1:9 (NIV)

I Bet You Didn't Know These Things About the Badge

Wearing the badge is an honor and a privilege. It comes with great determination, accomplishments, worthiness, stride, and struggles. As one who wears the badge, you will be watched, judged, tried, and tested because we are the face of a profession that everyone scrutinizes and criticizes.

Obtaining the badge is an honor, but keeping it requires you to have the right mindset and put in the work. Policing is a job where you can't pick the calls you will respond to or screen the individuals you encounter. It is a stressful occupation, and not everyone is built to endure the **stress,** outside forces, **criticism, judgements, opinions, and negativity plagues** of the job that the men and women in blue do their best to carry out while constantly being in the limelight.

Irene Reyes-Smith

As the face of law enforcement, the badge represents honor, integrity, and safety by the people who wear it. The badge has a way of making some individuals feel threatened, uneasy, and intimidated because of the power it gives the person wearing it. The profession is honored by many who believe officers will protect and make peace; however, there is a small percentage who dishonor the badge for one reason or another. I often ask myself, *what is it about the police that some individuals don't like?* Several reasons come to mind— one of them being what was ingrained in a person's mind when they were young about police.

While patrolling the streets, I have witnessed people and some parents point toward me and say to the child(ren), "I'm going to get that officer to lock you up," because the child was acting up or not doing as they were told. I would respond by telling the adult not to threaten them with the police because it sent the wrong message to child and gave a bad misrepresentation of officers. Some children grow up thinking the only interaction people have with police is when they are in trouble, which is not always the case. We must explain to our children the importance of authority and the need for them to grow up and become productive citizens in the world. Once they get older, they are held accountable for their actions, but once a foundation is laid, they will always remember it. There is no perfect child; however, we can help by providing guidance and making them aware that there are consequences behind your actions. After all, we want to see our children succeed in life, right?

Proverbs 22:6 (MSG) says, *point your kids in the right direction—when they're old they won't be lost.* The Amplified version states, *Train up a child in the way he should go [teaching him to seek God's wisdom and will for his abilities and talents], Even when he is old, he will not depart from it.* This means we must teach our children right from wrong. Show them how to live an exceptional life, teach them about Read the bible with them, teach them about God, show them how to live an exceptional life, and most importantly, teach them how to pray and pray with them. Our Lord tells us to pray without ceasing.

Authority is given from God; his word is clear in **Romans 13:1 (ESV):** *Let every person be subject to the governing authorities. For there is no authority except from God, and those that exist have been instituted by God.* No one is without sin, but your conduct, behavior, and actions of doing the right thing are what helps us to push forward and allows God to show us grace and mercy. I believe we can conquer all things together as a nation if everyone could just get on the same page. Everyone isn't born into wealth or have the same family dynamics and resources, but as individuals, we must use the God-given purpose and authority that has been placed inside of us to pursue and preserve what life brings to each of us. Remind yourself that you are stronger and wiser than what society says about you and claims you to be.

The word of God is clear, precise, and true. **Proverbs 3:5-6 (MSG)** says, *Trust God from the bottom of your heart; don't try to figure out everything on your own. Listen for God's voice in everything you do, everywhere you go; he's* *the one who will keep you on track.*

- **I Peter 5:6-7 (TLB)** *If you will humble yourselves under the mighty hand of God, in his good time he will lift you up. Let him have all your worries and cares, for he is always thinking about you and watching everything that concerns you.*

- **Philippians 4:13 (AMP)** *I can do all things [which He has called me to do] through Him who strengthens and empowers me [to fulfill His purpose–I am self-sufficient in Christ's sufficiency; I am ready for anything and equal to anything through Him who infuses me with inner strength and confident peace.]*

- **2 Timothy 3:16 (TLB)** *The whole Bible was given to us by inspiration from God and is useful to teach us what is true and to make us realize what is wrong in our lives; it straightens us out and helps us do what is right.*

We must ask ourselves what change we are looking for as citizens, police officers, politicians, communities, neighborhoods, society, and a nation. Everyone wants to see a change in policing, but no one wants to look within themselves and make the necessary changes. I'm sure we all agree that some things change with time. Well, so does everyone's mindset.

Law enforcement agencies nationwide have implemented policies, procedures, and practices of how officers must respond and react to various encounters, situations, and oppositions. Now more than ever, officers are challenged to perform the dynamics of calls for service while patrolling, communicating, and enforcing the laws in a society that questions the very **"badge"** we are speaking of.

Law enforcement responds to calls to assist citizens only to find out they are dealing with some of the same things in their life, such as family issues, children acting out, trials and challenges, etc. Policing is a profession where people feel officers can solve problems, issues, or situations at a moment's notice, but that is not always the case. Officers go to training and learn the laws of the land, but all situations are not the same. Some require more attention or resources than others. Some calls may even require the assistance of other agencies. Many people believe law enforcement agencies handle the majority of government services. Again, that's not the case. All agencies have to play their role in their prospective areas. The badge is a combination of trust, serenity, and service by an individual who took an oath to uphold and protect the law. However, when laws affect the process, position, and procedure of how policing is to be executive, it makes it hard for an officer to carry out their duties. In recent times, we have seen an increase in crime, especially concerning our youth, which has led to many asking what can be done to quell such incidences. What other policies can be put in place? How about more juvenile reform? What are the police doing to help? Where are the parents?

So many unanswered questions. My question is, what happened to the "It takes a village to raise a child" days?

When it comes to law enforcement's help, the truth is

there is a shortage of officers. They are exhausted from working long hours, resigning, and retiring early. As a result, police departments are implementing new strategies to attract the interest of new officers, such as sign-on bonuses, flexible days off, shortening the academy training, and even changing some of the criteria for becoming an officer. Although they still have to go through a background check, the person has a better chance of being hired now, resulting in individuals who probably wouldn't have applied before now applying for the job because of the incentives.

There is no other profession where the public constantly scrutinizes the actions of an employee and how they should provide or conduct service. Sometimes people forget officers deal with a lot, and constantly being looked at as a whole and not as an individual can be overwhelming. Officers get judged because of the uniform and the actions of co-workers. They get called out their names, spit on, and blamed because someone had a bad encounter with another officer. Where are the days when authority was respected? The crazy thing is we have heard individuals say not to do certain crimes or speed in Virginia because they don't play, but in the district, some individuals believe policing is a joke. They think they can do whatever they want because it's the atmosphere that has been established for this area. The real reason is they have taken so much authority from law enforcement agencies and officers that citizens and law violators believe they are in charge. Instead of working towards solutions that include the help of law enforcement, they tend to scrutinize the police and tell them how to do their job.

Law enforcement departments understand that policing is done in the eyes of the public. Still, when you have individuals who want to regulate and speak on every move an officer makes, it can become quite taxing for the men and women who work hard every day to ensure citizens, communities, and neighborhoods are safe.

Law enforcement agencies and policing look different across the nation. Some cities and states have different policies and procedures on how they manage their officers based on the demographics, neighborhoods, and communities they serve. Officers should never be judged by their race or ethnicity. Policing is a service provided by men and women who have taken an oath to do their best to uphold the law. **God** tells us, "All men are created equal," and we all were created in His image and likeness, no matter our status, ethnicity, or nationality. We are held accountable for our actions. So, regardless of an individual's background, living situation, or status quo, we must all treat everyone with RESPECT and LOVE.

It has gotten to where everything points back to police departments across the globe and not to the individuals plaguing the nation. The men and women in blue work countless hours, doing their best to offer protection. Officers are now more stressed. Their hands are sometimes tied, more crime is evolving, and no answers are in sight. The nation must come together even more now. The Bible speaks of these times in the book of **Revelation**—wars, rumors of wars, infectious diseases, crime, nations against nations, killing one another, and much more. God is not pleased, but the evilness is no surprise to **Him**. It's time to get prayer back in our schools.

The word of God tells us to pray without ceasing, which is pertinent to the chaos and turmoil plaguing our states, cities, communities, and even schools.

In my thirty-plus years of serving and protecting, I have never seen policing at this all-time low. We are in times where not everyone wants to discredit policing policies, but they do want to see some changes evolve. The village days need to resurface to get some form of normalcy in our communities. Our youth, neighborhoods, and streets need the help of everyone, and officers are necessary to keep peace, order, and safety. Everything can't be the police's fault. Some form of accountability must be taken for the actions that individuals put themselves in. Everyone must show more **empathy, love, kindness, and consideration** for others and themselves, regardless of ethnicity and race.

Why I Chose "Blue"

Just graduating high school, I was afforded the opportunity at a young age to join the nation's capital's finest police department, believing relating to the people and culture where you grew up is an extraordinary beginning.

I have a heart for serving. Yes, policing is a service, but I chose law enforcement because there was a need to help bring change in neighborhoods, communities, and society. Although it would seem practical to save everyone, helping one soul, one neighborhood, and one community at a time is just as good. I realized we must handle one call, one situation, and one problem at a time, addressing the need or circumstance at that moment. No two calls are the same. The call may involve the same individuals but not be the same situation as before. People in dire need of assistance may not realize that sometimes it is not a police matter. The situation may require the help of another agency.

I started in the 90s when crime was at its highest, and now, in the 2000s, history is almost repeating itself. We must collectively come together to see how change can be implemented. I grew up in the era when teachers could paddle you in school, and when you got home, your parents would handle the rest of your punishment. We respected our parents, seniors, authority, and teachers back then and asked no questions. Children were taught to be seen and not heard. I'm not sure if that was a good thing, but that's what it was. You knew that whatever was said by an adult was best for you at the time. We knew certain things would not be tolerated or accepted because there would be repercussions later.

After a while, I wanted to do something in the field that involved helping our youth. It is an area most overlooked, and the help is much needed. I started working in community outreach and understood the support our youth needed. The mission of community outreach was to engage, interact, and express the collaboration between the officers and community while helping with the needs of the residents and neighborhoods. We would block off the streets in various neighborhoods during the summer and have police interactions and fun activities, such as rope jumping, grilling hot dogs, arts & crafts, hopscotch, dodgeball, and much more. We called it "Playstreets." The residents and parents loved it because some kids did not attend camp and were home with nothing to do. So, we were that connection to assist the parents. These activities would take place Monday through Friday during the day in the summer months when school was out. The holidays were exciting, as well. We would partner with different organizations to make sure the families in need had the support, supplies, and sanctity they needed during these times.

In 2007, I transitioned to work in truancy, which involved more interaction and direct contact to support our youth. Truancy was one of the most challenging times in my career, as encounters with our youth were never easy. We would go to houses to speak to the parents and the child only to find out they didn't want to attend school for various reasons and situations. Some were dealing with being bullied, had no uniforms, not enough food, lost their bus pass to get back and forth, or didn't have the school materials needed. Some children even refused to go to school because their family couldn't afford to dress them in designer shoes like some of the other students wore.

We understand not all situations or issues affect all youth and students, but for the ones it does, the school systems or administrators can't or aren't aware of them all. We would go to schools to do pop-up visits for some of the truant youth, and to our surprise, they were happy and puzzled to see we were checking up on them. Children like structure, and the fact that we visited their schools showed them the police care about them and their well-being. The administrators would tell us that some parents hadn't been to the school since back-to-school night to find out how their child was progressing, if at all, or if they were attending school on a regular basis. Kids need to feel loved and know they belong. We understand life happens, and then there are work demands, but our youth and children are the future. If we don't pour, guide, or assist them now, we will be visiting them in jail or the morgue later. **Real talk!** The reality is there is no handbook on parenting. We must come together to help, assist, and guide our youth with their mindset change, along with the family structure to develop a more solid community and neighborhoods.

The peer pressure that plagues some of our youth today is real and challenging for them. Social media plays another huge part in their life. Most times, people only show the best of their life, and when this is exposed to our children. It has them thinking they can live the same way. It's time to take back the lives of our children and youth. As the word of the Lord says, "Train them up in the way they should go." I'm not saying they won't have trials, tribulations, oppositions, or obstacles, but God would order their steps, and they would see His hand working in their life.

I am certain all professions have their challenges, issues, and obstacles, but officers get called to them all. Sometimes it's beyond our control and scope of work, but we are left to handle it. From time to time, my partner and I would buy breakfast, give money for bus passes, purchase uniforms, and provide lunch money to those kids who needed such. I have responded to calls at CVS pharmacies during school hours where kids were stealing food and other items because they hadn't had anything to eat and didn't have money to buy food. Some parents just didn't have it. Officers try their best to find help and provide resources for individuals and families who need help.

Truancy really touched my heart because of some of our youths' lifestyles and living conditions. Some barely have any food, and some have little supervision at home, but many deal with other obstacles.

I remember when we were called to an elementary school for an incident. Upon arriving at the school, we were met by an administrator and led to the classroom of a kindergarten teacher, who advised that a kindergartner had kicked her. My eyes got BIG, and I said, "What?!" After she repeated herself, my partner and I looked at each other and then asked the teacher where the student was. We spoke with the child and explained they were never to kick a teacher or any other adult for that matter. (If I can be honest, I wanted to tell the child to kick me and see what would happen, but I knew that wouldn't be appropriate.) The parents arrived and were so apologetic, wanting to know the next course of action. We explained there would have to be mediation with them, the teacher, and the school administration.

There is still a need for village building to help raise children and youth in a society where some of them feel extremely entitled and fear nothing. The word of God is clear that He didn't give us the spirit of FEAR but of LOVE and a sound mind! With that said, we must express to them that life is precious. They need to cherish it and live purposefully. We must teach our children at a young age to respect authority and obey their parents so they may have a long life on Earth.

I have witnessed youth homelessness for one reason or another. That should not be. We are living in times where everyone is trying their best to survive and thrive. The pandemic has changed the way we work, live, and function to a degree. The family dynamics did get closer in some instances but still has some way to go. Some have experienced the loss of their job, a decrease in their salary, or a position change. The life of our youth has to be a priority. As a nation, we must come together and implement a way to help single mothers raise their young boys, teen moms who are uncertain how to care for their young child, and, lastly, bridge the gap between the police and communities.

Sometimes officers wonder what's the best way is to handle certain situations concerning children. I remember an incident involving truancy where my partner and I stopped a young lady not in school during school hours. We introduced ourselves as Truancy Officers and asked why she wasn't in school. When the young lady didn't reply, we repeated the question. She finally responded, "Because I'm not. I'm going to the library." We then told her that she couldn't be in the library during school hours. Upon asking her what school she attended, she decided she wanted to kick me in my knee with some boots she had on, causing me immense pain. My first instinct was to grab her, and just as I was attempting to, the officers on scene called my name, stopping me in my tracks. In a furious voice, I asked her, "Why did you kick me? All we wanted to know is why you weren't in school." That's when she stated, "I'm suspended," to which I replied, "And now you're going to jail for assault." She apologized and pleaded with us not to take her to jail. Of course, I didn't mean it. We called her mother and explained the situation, and she was so apologetic and concerned about her daughter's behavior towards us. That interaction could have gone a different way had she been respectful when asked why she was not in school. This situation was another example of not adhering to authority and answering the questions asked.

Unfortunately, I had to have surgery, where they had to cut open my leg and reposition my dislocated kneecap that had shifted from the force of the kick. My recovery was long and rehab intense. I endured being pushed around in a wheelchair and walking on crutches. The physical challenges and not knowing if or when I would be able to return to work played a lot on my mental state. All of this because she didn't want to answer the question and decided to kick an officer in full uniform. This was the most uncertain and challenging time in my entire career. The situation didn't have to go that way had she been cooperative, but the damage was done. We have to make sure we instill in our children at a young age the consequences of their actions. I still have pain in that knee today!

The profession comes with the possibility of severe accidents and injuries to officers, but no one wants to be a victim of abuse—not citizens and surely not officers. Several officers get hurt throughout their career. Some make it back, and some don't. For those who don't, that is the end of their career. Policing is a profession where there is a possibility of some injuries, even death. Still, officers don't expect to intentionally be hurt or harmed just because someone doesn't like the police.

Irene Reyes-Smith

The profession of a law enforcement officer is great. You get the opportunity to help individuals and make a difference in a positive way, assisting someone with change or helping them complete some goals or aspirations in their life. My experiences helped me see that neighborhoods, communities, and society must work together to accomplish what is best for the nation to thrive.

The Metropolitan Police Department is a unique organization. I'm not saying that just because I was employed there but because it serves the nation's capital and all its entities. MPDC is the face when organizations want to protest, march, have parades, and express their freedom of speech in other ways. The members of this department protect and serve its residents and visitors to the fullest. No department is perfect, just as no individual is perfect, but MPDC takes pride in the work that the men and women in blue honor. I hope we can get to a place where everyone respects human life and authority and positively fulfills their purpose on Earth.

Things You Will Never Understand About the Badge

Imagine what the people wearing the uniform encounter every second, hour, and day of their shift while performing their job duties. Policing is not a nine-to-five operation, as some may think. The majority of operations are twenty-four hours a day every day. Your mind and heart must be in it, or else this isn't the profession for you. Officers have bad days, get discouraged, feel under the weather, face family issues, and still must maintain professionalism. They are always in the public's eye and often criticized.

Police are misjudged by many. Some individuals hardly take the time to greet officers, let alone check their well-being. At the end of the day, we are all human beings. The long days (10, 12, and 18 hours) can affect an officer's mind, body, and soul. The life of an officer is only understood by other officers or those in law enforcement.

Some individuals may have wanted to become a police officer but are now having second thoughts because of so much controversy in the nation. The reality is officers understand no one should lose their life while interacting with law enforcement. Life is precious on both sides, and as a society, we must search deep within ourselves to ensure we display humanity! God's word is clear in **Psalms 51:10 (ESV):** *Create in me a clean heart, O God, and renew a right spirit within me.* God's word also says in **Jeremiah 17:10 (NLT):** *But I, the Lord, search all hearts and examine secret motives. I give all people their due rewards, according to what their actions deserve."*

The ones in power try to accommodate people who want to exercise their rights to freedom of speech and freedom to peaceful protest, parades, marches, outside gatherings, and marathons. However, these events have to be secured by the police. They are not always the most pleasant, peaceful, or positive events, but officers must do them for however many hours are needed. So, when the thought or discussion arises of defunding the police and abolishing some policing duties, remember that officers are the ones to arrive when called to protect people, neighborhoods, communities, and groups from those individuals who set out to destroy, interrupt events, and cause hostile situations and environments.

The defunding movement was the start of a safety concern for everyone. Law enforcement nationwide wasn't sure how or what to expect from this, but society, citizens, and the government needed some sort of strategies, solutions, and safety measures in place. Most government agencies assisting law enforcement departments with certain calls or crises are not a twenty-hour operation. Therefore, when the question was raised about **utilizing mental health workers, psychiatrists, and social workers** to assist with emergency situations, there was a lot of pushbacks because their operations didn't extend until the late night and early morning hours as policing does. The idea may have been a great one, but the fact remains that first responders are the only ones who work around the clock.

An officer can't wholly go on what they see! When they arrive at a scene, they have to focus on what aligns with the law they have studied, learned, and know. After many years of working in law enforcement, I realized only what I did for Christ will last, even while doing my job. I didn't have to look down on individuals, treat them less than, or belittle them because of my authority. The "**BADGE'** holds much power but should not be misused. The power comes from our Lord and Savior, who gives us the ability to accomplish all He has for us to do in our purpose-filled lives and professions.

After many years of responding to calls day in and day out, I realized all people sometimes want is for someone to hear them out and show concern for the issues at that moment. Sometimes citizens don't understand that officers don't always have the time to analyze and engage in long conversations. An officer tries to rectify the situation with the best solution. Some calls and scenes are more hectic than others and can't be immediately solved. Some situations require more time, and sometimes officers have to get a supervisor involved.

Law enforcement agencies have put in place tools, resources, and programs that help citizens better understand the life of being a police officer, one being the **Ride-Along Program.** With this program, the public can come during a shift and ride with an officer. It allows citizens to witness what a law enforcement officer has to deal with or come in contact with on a day-to-day basis. How many of you have taken advantage of this opportunity to see what a day in policing is like? I remember having a ride-along, and by the end of the shift, the individual stated, "You can have this. There is no way I could do this job." I responded, saying, "Yes, it's a lot, but someone has to do it." Afterwards, they had a better understanding and regard for officers and the profession.

The job of a law enforcement officer is not easy. It may look like it is, but contrary to belief, it takes a toll on your mind and body. Officers are not robots. We are human beings who have feelings. We laugh, cry, bleed, and hurt, but we keep on going because it is what we signed up for when we took the oath. I love the resilience of the men and women in blue. Sadly, the commitment, concern, and consistency officers demonstrate are more times overlooked than acknowledged.

Law enforcement officers deal with so many internal issues within their perspective departments that sometimes they are unsure which way to turn or who to seek help from. Society has demanded so much from law enforcement agencies that it has put a strain on the men and women who serve in this profession day in and day out. The streets are one kind of stress, but when coming to work every day and finding out there is another change, more training, and new policies, it starts to weigh on the mental, physical, and social of an officer after a while. Society has it that now policing is being questioned from every angle. Police are not counselors. They are not judges, schoolteachers, lawyers, politicians, physiatrists, or lawmakers. They enforce the law but instead are held to a standard for all these professions mentioned. We take on some of these roles and do our best to handle the circumstances or situations. Imagine rising early in the morning and going to work when most people are still sleeping. Once there, you get your assignment and then off to the streets you go, not knowing what you will be up against at any given moment on any given day. They understand it comes with the territory, though.

Most people know what their job will entail daily, but that's not the case in law enforcement. No two days are the same. Those who work office jobs usually have assigned offices or workspaces and scheduled hours with an ending time for their workday. Officers do not. Officers may or may not get off on time, depending on what is taking place. The days can be long, and sometimes your days off are taken away. Some may not even make it home. Only God knows the outcome. Officers have spouses who want them home, children who need them, and families who want to spend time with them. Family means a lot to the women and men in blue, and the demands of their job can affect the mind, body, and spirit of everyone.

Irene Reyes-Smith

Imagine being an officer who is a single parent and raising your child with little assistance. While at work, you find out you must stay and work an extra shift. There may be protestors causing disturbances, a riot breaking out, or another act of crime that requires all hands-on deck. However, you don't have anyone to pick up your child when school lets out. What do you do? Who do you call? These are some of the situations officers must face concerning family matters on a weekly or monthly basis. Officers understand the risk and demands of the job, but they sometimes ask themselves: *Do I have children now or wait? Do I pursue marriage now or wait until I'm closer to the end of my career? Do I start a family now? Do I stay on the job?* The life of an officer can be complicated physically, mentally, and emotionally. The average citizen wouldn't understand the defeats, dishonesty, disconnect, and downpouring officers face at any given time.

What Happens When the "Blue" Crosses the Line

In today's society, we are outraged with the deaths of individuals by police, but crimes with our youth and adults killing one another almost seem to be normalized. A life is a life, and yes, officers are held to a higher standard. When are we going to come together as a nation to value human life? After all, **God** created us equal and in **His** image.

Law enforcement agencies across the nation have taken a turn, and officers are left scratching and shaking their heads, beginning with the defunding of the police movement, which was not looked at across the board. When one department is singled out, it affects all law enforcement agencies, even if they are not the target. The **Defund the Police** movement was a cry out for justice and changes, but no one really thought about what that would be like or how it would affect law enforcement agencies nationwide. All police departments aren't dealing with the same issues, criticism, or injustices. When you take away daily duties from officers and police departments, you chip away at policing. Now, officers are more stressed, their hands are tied, more crime is evolving, and no answers are in sight. The nation has to come together. The Bible speaks of these times in the book of **Revelation**—wars, infectious diseases, crime, killing one another, and much more. God is not pleased with the evil taking place, and it's time TO PRAY The Bible states in **Romans 12:12 (TLB):** *Be glad for all God is planning for you. Be patient in trouble, and prayerful always.*

In my thirty-plus years of serving and protecting, I have never seen policing at its all-time low. Policing has many components, and officers are often misunderstood and underappreciated. The time is now to make the changes and come together. Officers should have a say in implementing changes since this will ultimately affect them and how police duties should be carried out. Officers try their best to do what is necessary to ensure everyone is safe and compliant. At times, it can be challenging because we live in times where mental health is on the rise and **RESPECT** for authority has changed. Respect comes from the heart and should be taught at a young age. Respect goes both ways.

The Bible speaks on authority in **Romans 13:1-5 (MSG):** *Be a good citizen. All governments are under God. Insofar as there is peace and order, it's God's order. So live responsibly as a citizen. If you're irresponsible to the state,* *then you're irresponsible with God, and God will hold you responsible. Duly constituted authorities are only a threat if you're trying to get by with something. Decent citizens should have nothing to fear.*

Do you want to be on good terms with the government? Be a responsible citizen and you'll get on just fine, the government working to your advantage. But if you're breaking the rules right and left, watch out. The police aren't there just to be admired in their uniforms. God also has an interest in keeping order, and he uses them to do it. That's why you must live responsibly—not just to avoid punishment but also because it's the right way to live.

We are human, and sometimes things happen. But God's word is clear and precise.

The Bible is a guide to our steps, our souls, and our security. We must teach our children about prayer and the power it has! God is still able to do exceedingly above all we can ask, think, or imagine according to His riches in Glory! The Bible is God's words for us to follow!

The Bible:
- Basic
- Instructions
- Before
- Leaving
- Earth

The Bible states, "Many are called, but few are chosen." Peacemakers are chosen, but challenges are inevitable. The word of the Lord tells us in **Jeremiah 29:11(NIV):** *For I* *know the plans I have for you," declares the Lord, "plans to prosper you and not to harm you, plans to give you hope and a future.* The Lord gives a plan and hope to those officers who take the oath of honor to do good.

Policing is a profession many believe is called, but you must know within your **HEART** that it's in you because one wrong move, decision, lack of attention, and attitude can affect your life or someone else's. Some believe policing will give them the power, authority, or self-pride to make people **respect** them. These individuals have often been bullied, taken advantage of, or not taken seriously, which are all wrong reasons for wanting to become a police officer. If not managed properly, a person will abuse the power of the badge, resulting in officers being looked at in a negative light by the public.

In the last couple of years, we have seen a series of events where policing has not been positive in the public's eye—one being the deaths of several young black men killed by interacting with police officers. It has been a long, hard journey for communities, neighborhoods, parents, officers, and families. The solution is not easy and will take the collaboration of everyone coming together to understand the roles we all play in these encounters. Yes, police are trained to protect and serve, but when there is no compassion, love, empathy, and control, you're operating in something else that cannot be trained. Officers must look from within because that is where change comes from, and there is no training for self-evaluation. Officers must ask themselves: *Am I going to be the change needed? Am I going to be the one who believes policing is for me? Will I make a difference in policing?*

Secondly, as a society, we cannot continue allowing race to be a factor in our decision-making, moves, or actions. We cannot continue to allow violence in our neighborhoods or communities. We must step up and make the change needed.

I often hear people say the police only come around when someone gets shot. The reality is residents are the eyes and ears of the police because they can't be everywhere all the time.

Law enforcement departments across the nation receive almost the same training. Still, as it relates to each state in policing and policies, there are differences in the demographics, culture, and politics. The question remains, **what can be done? How can we affect change in policing?** After working for so many years, you have a level of **caution, care, and concern** for your actions. I believe we all have opinions, comments, concerns, approaches, and appreciation for policing, but when circumstances, situations, or things don't line up with how someone's view or perspective of an officer's action should be, then we see and hear defund, more reform, take away certain aspects of officers' duties, and more training. The truth is that many police departments have made reforms and changes to policies and are holding officers responsible who stand around and watch other officers violate the law and someone's rights. No one sees or wants to see when individuals commit crimes and feel they can do whatever needs to be done to elude police or try to turn the scene into a fiasco to get attention. God created us all in His image and likeness, so it shouldn't matter whether someone's skin color is lighter or darker than yours. The facts are the facts. Crime is crime, and it shouldn't matter who committed it. Unfortunately, in some instances and calls, it does.

The fact remains that officers, citizens, and politicians must continue to look within themselves and examine what's inside. Then ask yourself, *AM I THE BEST ME I CAN BE? AM I UTILIZING WHAT GOD HAS PLACED IN ME TO THE BEST OF MY ABILITY?*

Lessons:
- Policing is a job that can have you up at night wondering if you did the best, you could do that day.
- Did you serve the residents and community to the best of your ability?
- Did you do your due diligence to honor your department today?
- Did you save a life or impact one today or at any time throughout your career?
- What could you have done differently when responding to calls today?
- What impression did you leave on someone today?
- Do you have the right mindset for the job?

These are the questions you should ask yourself from time to time during re-evaluation and reflection.

When Society and Policing Don't Agree

Where are the politicians and activists when our young black African American men are killing one another? A parent having to bury their child(ren) due to gun violence should not be the norm. The double standards that exist have to stop. A life is a life! When someone is killed during an interaction with the police, everyone wants to protest, riot, and yell, "Black Lives Matter!" However, when our youth and young black men gun each other down on the streets, a blind eye is turned to some degree. Sadly, it seems society has gotten numb to the shootings and killings. As a nation, we have to put a stop to ALL killings, not just the ones we think should be addressed.

Everyone has to play a part in getting the village back, but it's hard when people are quick to say it's not their child. Some parents don't seem to care until their child becomes a statistic. I understand raising kids today is hard, especially with so many outside negative influences. Social media is raising some of our youth, and rap songs glorify drugs, sex, and violence. In addition, there are a plethora of single mothers who desperately need help raising their children to stay on the straight and narrow path. There is a lack of structure in many households. There is no manual for parenting, but as parents, you must realize it is okay to ask for help and seek God, who said he would never leave us nor forsake us. Children are a blessing from the Lord, and God does not give us more than we can bear! We just must call on Him, day and night. We must get back to one nation under God!

People want the police to help drive out crime in their neighborhood, but when law enforcement stakes out the hot zones and high crime sections, they question why they are posted on the corners and not cruising around catching the criminals. What they don't understand is that the mere presence of the police can deter those types of individuals. Let me make something clear. I am not saying everyone is against the police, but at the same time, please realize officers can't always be everywhere all the time. We need the people's help. Citizens can be the eyes and ears when officers are not around in their communities or neighborhoods and speak up, communicating to the officers the wrongdoing they witness. It is time for everyone to do their part so that we can all live a **happy, healthy, and honorable life.**

The time has come to put it out there. Not only are

citizens fed up with the unjust treatment and biases, but officers see it, as well, when responding to a home and are told by the resident that they wanted an officer of a different race to assist them. Some people even request that the officer responds to the rear or service door of the residence. The disrespect, biased acts, and prejudiced behaviors were all actions of individual citizens that needed police assistance.

We still have a long way to go to display freedom for all. Officers are faced attitudes and behavior from citizens just because they are doing their job. The lack of respect today towards humankind is appalling, but the fact remains that because officers have taken an oath to serve the public, they must conduct themselves accordingly regardless. Stop and ask yourself if this behavior is warranted toward officers. Some people feel officers are to adhere to what they want from them rather than what is lawful and legal. Officers are not your personal security guard.

Some feel that because of their financial status and where they live, it is their right and entitlement to get whatever they desire or need from the police departments in their area, community, or neighborhood. In certain locations, police patrol heavily, such as in high-crime areas and places with heavy drug trafficking activities. Whereas other regions do not require the constant presence of police because the individuals doing the crimes or drug activities have different tactics for their incognito criminal activities. We understand illegal activities and crime must be addressed, but the tactics and procedures of doing things are **relevant!**

The service of law enforcement doesn't mean either side can do as they please. Citizens and officers must be governed by the law— both the law of the land and the word of God.

Policing shouldn't see color, just a human being! At the end of it all, we are all God's children. It's true no one wants to mix politics and religion, but God's word is the missing piece (peace) that will cure and connect us all. God brought this scripture to mind—**John 14:27 (AMP)**: Peace, I leave with you; My [perfect] peace I give to you; not as the world gives do I give to you. Do not let your heart be troubled, nor let it be afraid. [Let My perfect peace calm you in every circumstance and give you courage and strength for every challenge.]

Do You Know the Officer Behind the Badge?

An officer's day starts with them attending roll call and getting their assignment for the day, which can change at a moment's notice depending on the circumstances or situations that arise throughout the workday. Officers are assigned to patrol areas where they encounter and interact with citizens daily. The question remains, do you know the officer behind the badge? The reality is most citizens don't know who the officers are that patrol their neighborhood or community.

I believe communication between officers and civilians should not only occur when the police are responding to a call or coming to a person(s) aide. Being courteous and polite goes a long way. For some reason, society believes they are not supposed to interact with law enforcement officers unless it's in times of emergencies, but that is not true. Communication should not only be when you or someone you know is in trouble, involved in a family disturbance, or during a traffic stop. Try wishing an officer a good morning. Ask how they are doing and/or how their day is going. These statements go a long way with an officer and can help to build better relationships between officers and society.

Many small things can be done to bridge the gap and start dialogue between officers and the community. A daily hello, a smile when crossing paths, a thank you, expressing appreciation, showing respect, and being non-judgmental are just a few ways to break down barriers on both sides. We must realize that we all need each other in some form or another.

The stereotypes placed on officers based on individuals' opinions have made it difficult to establish relationships between the community and police, which is crucial during these times we are currently living in.

The Bible speaks on authority and judging in John 7:24:

Look beneath the surface so you can judge correctly."

(New Living Translation)

Do not judge by appearance [superficially and arrogantly], but judge fairly and righteously."

(Amplified Bible)

Stop judging according to outward appearances; rather judge according to righteous judgement."

(Christian Standard Bible)

This scripture speaks to all of us individually and collectively as a society and nation. We have all judged at some point in our life. The time has come for us to see everyone as children of God that he created to be equal and live in harmony. The authority to the government and police was given by God, which is upon his shoulders to make sure laws, rules, and peaceful living is carried out.

Communities and neighborhoods are hurting. Knowing this, officers search for solutions, and knowing the officer behind the badge can help them to help you. It can begin healing the severely damaged relationship between police and civilians. Many officers have taken steps to establish relationships with the people in the communities they serve. They listen to the residents and communicate with business owners in the neighborhoods they patrol.

Contrary to popular belief, if an officer can help one person throughout their day, it brings them joy. Many law enforcement officers throughout the nation are genuinely concerned with what happens in the communities and neighborhoods where they serve despite what may have been seen or heard in the media and the opinion people have formed about them. Many of us have family members who work in law enforcement, and therefore, we know their character. Keeping this in mind, ask yourself the following:

- **Would you be willing to share a positive encounter you had with the police if there's the chance it could change someone else's negative opinion?**

- Will you judge an officer based on someone else's experience?
- Do you believe officers have no feelings or empathy?
- Do you know the officer behind the badge?

Seasoned Men in Blue

The following stories are the experiences of retired officer Ronald Hampton and active member Chief of Police Marcus Jones. Things are constantly evolving in law enforcement. Not to mention, the years an officer serves his community plays a part in how they police. So, enjoy reading the experiences of these two "men in blue" as they give you more insight and a different perspective on how officers were during their era of policing.

Retired Officer
Ronald Hampton

From 1971 to 1994, I served in the DC Metropolitan Police Department. My story begins at the end of my service in the US Air Force, 1967–1971. Upon exiting the military, I worked on Capitol Hill for a senator from Virginia. However, that did not last long. A friend of mine, who was serving in the DC Police Department, thought I would find a career in law enforcement interesting. Frankly, I didn't think much of the suggestion, especially with my awareness of the racial issues in the city. We were coming out of the rebellions of the late 1960s, and I had experienced several unpleasant racial incidents in Vietnam and my last duty station at Dover Air Force Base in Dover, Delaware.

After several days of contemplation, I decided to take the test, which I passed. I then proceeded to the DC Police and Fire Clinic to finish the next step of the process after being scheduled. Once I completed the mental and physical examinations, I started preparing myself to be a police officer. About two weeks passed, and I received a letter in the mail. The DC Metropolitan Police Department rejected me because I have a metal pin in my right elbow. The pin was put in my elbow at the age of thirteen to repair a cracked bone from playing football. Even though I had served in the US Air Force and fought in a war so we could be free, I was rejected from serving in the police service, which is nothing compared to being in the military. So, I reached out to a lawyer and doctor because I had concluded if I could join the US Air Force and go to war to defend my country, I could be a police officer in Washington, DC.

After several consultations with medical and legal experts, they issued a letter to the DC Metropolitan Police Department stating the pin in my right elbow would not prevent me from carrying out the duties of a police officer. That was the beginning of my experience as a police officer in DC.

At the conclusion of my medical, physical, and mental examination, there was no space in the academic for a new class. So, I and others were assigned around the department in the meantime. I was assigned to the Identification and Records Division for about two weeks until I was finally told to report to the academy, where a new class would start for the recruits.

Our class was selected to participate in a different learning model then. The standard class was usually taught using the instructor model in classrooms. However, our class used a pre and post-test model, which involved taking a pre-test, then reading the material and taking a post-test. The model also required us to score 85% or better on the post-test and academic classroom material.

The academic experiences involved several tension-filled moments with our classroom officers and required us to be there from 7:00 am until 4:00 pm. They kept us busy most of the day with physical conditioning, studies, and other training-related activities. While in training, we were informed which district or unit we would be assigned. I was assigned to the Third District—the beginning of a new and sometimes unbelievable set of experiences.

Montgomery County's Chief of Police, Marcus Jones

Power is vested upon police officers by local, state, and federal laws. It provides these trusted individuals to enforce the laws of the land and keep the peace in communities. Power is defined in Merriam-Webster Dictionary as a possession of control, authority, or influence of others. Thus, the trust provided to these badged individuals with a gun and authority is supposed to be deemed with a higher level of integrity than most professions in America. Yet, the human beings granted such control and influence have the ability to earn or destroy trust with either positive or negative utilization of the given power.

Over the centuries, there has been an opportunity to develop positive relationships with the communities that police officers swear to protect. There has been a basic premise of developing relationships with individuals or groups of people to create an atmosphere of protection with honor and pride. The ability to serve the public and be given this incredible amount of authority should be treated with the utmost respect.

The profession is noted as potentially dangerous; it is clearly understood that one will place themselves in danger's way and may have to lay down their life for others, which undoubtedly is the ultimate sacrifice. Therefore, many citizens recognize and respect this possibility as well as the other aspects of the profession, which creates a basic trust of the officers in most communities. Officers can show the human side of themselves behind the badge by being personable, developing strong relationships, and demonstrating kindness, passion, and empathy. These attributes assist with the positive nature of policing, and many citizens often never forget these officers due to the relationships developed. This positive power provides the best opportunity to gain and maintain trust among the communities that law enforcement officers serve.

Police officers have proven to create positive relationships that have led to positive outcomes. Policing has evolved in some ways to build more distinctive relationships with faith communities, seniors, children, and groups with disabilities, as a few examples. When policing has been identified as a need to assist with protecting groups, such as noted above, it allows for the opportunity to put forth the actions of the police officers through those relationships to obtain the goals of serving with positive power. This has been proven when parents of autistic children are introduced to a police program in Montgomery County, Maryland, which assists them with information on how to handle situations when their child may be missing. The parents see how officers are trained to identify children with autism and how to handle them sensitively if they locate them. There are also examples of faith communities requesting assistance for security protection and police departments guiding them with safety plans. Positive youth programs, such as the Police Athletic League, have produced positive outcomes in communities where it has been needed the most, and individuals who experienced it provide positive reflections to show how it impacted their lives.

The aspect of policing centers around many facets in our community, and the opportunities are extensive to provide positive outcomes and, most importantly, to build trust.

Policing in communities across this land has long been corrupted by individual and groups of police officers who have utilized their powers in a selfish, greedy, and superior manner. Crimes involving police officers have ranged from murder to bribes, to dealing drugs and protecting drug dealers, to excessive use of force and authority, to name just a few. These individuals who convinced hiring officials and directors of law enforcement agencies that they were the best person for the job and wanted to help people feel safe in the community made a concerted effort at some point in their careers to change from a positive path to the land of corruption and destruction. These officers with a badge of authority took a stance of bullying people in communities and utilizing excessive force while falsifying reports and lying on the witness stand to obtain convictions of the innocent. These are those who used the power of their authority negatively to destroy the trust of those they were sworn to protect. Communities of color, particularly the Black community, have been trampled by law enforcement in our history by utilizing the negative power to accomplish their heavy-handed goals of the end justifying the means.

As Irene Reyes-Smith explores the story behind the badge, it gives us all the understanding that the power instilled upon our law enforcement officers—both past and present—has been and is currently looked upon with skepticism and lack of faith in the performance of individuals in government.

The presence of power means an inherited trust of individuals in all phases of government, and the police profession is among those with the highest standards. Hiring humans with the utmost ethical behavior and maintaining the highest level of integrity will be one of the essential keys to developing and maintaining trust for those who wear the badge. The power vested in these individuals who demonstrate integrity, trust, and honor will help the badge shine bright. Any negative power associated with this privilege will only make its appearance dull.

Conclusion

It is my hope you now have a better understanding of **The Badge.** This book provided a brief breakdown of what the badge represents and the power it and the officers who wear it hold. As time progresses, I believe society, communities, neighborhoods, authorities, and officers will collaborate, connect, and communicate more about how we should govern together to make the necessary adjustments in life and within ourselves to achieve a better outlook on each other's role. The God we serve does exceedingly and abundantly above what we can ask, think, or imagine.

Even though it's a symbol that holds much **significance, power, and authority,** **the badge** can be of help to everyone. Officers nationwide just want peace and order from everyone. The truth behind the matter is that everyone has a part to play. No one entity can do it alone, and we as a people must stop thinking that everything should be on the shoulders of law enforcement. The time has come that we can't continue the name-blame game and must call these elected officials out of their comfort zone to do what needs to be done to help our families and youth. I believe everyone—regardless of their race—can benefit from a happy, healthy lifestyle if given the same resources, opportunities, guidance, and help. We must continue to walk by Faith. Remember, if God is before us, who can be against us? **NO ONE!**

Thank you for the support of this book and know that the word of God is still our guide. Only what you do for **Christ** will last!

Acknowledgements

I want to give all glory to Jesus, who gave me the vision for this book and provided the resources, my mindset, and the information obtained to publish it.

Sincere appreciation—but never forgotten— to my parents, Jose and Ana Reyes, who have gone on to Glory. I love you so much and miss you dearly.

I want to give honor and thanks to my hubby for being an important part of this project. So grateful for him always. Love you!

To my family, I am so grateful to you for the support you have shown me. I know you will always be there for me, and I appreciate each of you in your own individual way. Thanks so much.

My appreciation to Ron Hampton for his contribution, sharing his law enforcement journey while policing in unprecedented times.

My deepest thanks to Marcus Jones, Montgomery County's Chief of Police, who shared his concerns and comments regarding the "badge" worn by men and women across the nation.

Irene Reyes-Smith

Last but certainly not least, to Charron Monaye, Founder and CEO of Pen Legacy, for another opportunity to allow my thoughts and ideas to be seen and read by the world. Thanks for your push, persistence, and publishing expertise. Such a joy to work with you always.

Your Thoughts...

Have you had a positive experience with police?
If so, did you share it with someone else?

_____

_____

_____

_____

_____

_____

_____

_____

_____

_____

_____

_____

Irene Reyes-Smith

What is your view of the badge?

_____

_____

_____

_____

_____

_____

_____

_____

_____

_____

_____

_____

_____

_____

_____

What does the badge represent to you?

_____

_____

_____

_____

_____

_____

_____

_____

_____

_____

_____

_____

_____

_____

_____

_____

_____

_____

Irene Reyes-Smith

How do you see officers who wear the badge?

_____

_____

_____

_____

_____

_____

_____

_____

_____

_____

_____

_____

_____

_____

_____

Where can the gap be bridged between police
and communities?

_____

_____

_____

_____

_____

_____

_____

_____

_____

_____

_____

_____

_____

_____

How can generations come together?

What does unity look like to you?

_____

_____

_____

_____

_____

_____

_____

_____

_____

_____

_____

_____

_____

_____

_____

_____

_____

Irene Reyes-Smith

What do you think it will take for some people to look at the police as helpful instead of harmful?

_____

_____

_____

_____

_____

_____

_____

_____

_____

_____

_____

_____

_____

_____

_____

How can you change someone's perspective in life about policing?

_____

_____

_____

_____

_____

_____

_____

_____

_____

_____

_____

_____

_____

_____

_____

Irene Reyes-Smith

What does police reform look like to you?

_____

_____

_____

_____

_____

_____

_____

_____

_____

_____

_____

_____

_____

_____

_____

_____

Why do you feel police reform is needed?

_____

_____

_____

_____

_____

_____

_____

_____

_____

_____

_____

_____

_____

_____

_____

_____

_____

Ask yourself if you exemplify part of the problem or solutions when protecting your community. How so?

_____

_____

_____

_____

_____

_____

_____

_____

_____

_____

_____

_____

_____

_____

www.ingramcontent.com/pod-product-compliance
Lightning Source LLC
Chambersburg PA
CBHW040908210326
41597CB00029B/5013

* 9 7 9 8 9 8 8 5 8 0 6 5 2 *